# Perfume & Cigarettes

## Madeline Levy

Top Shelf Poetry Series #5

Six Ft. Swells Press

After Hours Poetry

*Perfume & Cigarettes*
Copyright 2015 © Madeline Levy

Top Shelf Poetry Series #5
Six Ft. Swells Press
www.AfterHoursPoetry.com
www.facebook.com/SixFtSwells

Editors: Todd Cirillo, Julie Valin, Matt Amott
Cover Photo: Todd Cirillo
Beauty provided by: Madeline Levy
Book & Cover Design: Julie Valin, The Word Boutique,
www.TheWordBoutique.net

Acknowledgements:
"Bird's Got my Dream" previously published in *Poeming Pigeons* and Six Ft. Swells website; "Why I Meet You at Midnight" previously published in *Lummox Press Anthology*.

All rights reserved.
Printed in the United States of America.
No part of this book may be reproduced in any manner without written permission except in the case of brief quotations included in critical essays, reviews and articles.

ISBN 13:   978-0-9853075-4-7
ISBN 10:   0985307544

*To my mom, who always encouraged me to let
my freak flag fly; whose mantras—
"fuck 'em if they can't take a joke", and
"when in doubt, do the friendly thing"—
taught me to be unapologetically goofy and kind.*

°o₀

# The Scenic Route . . .

| | |
|---|---|
| No Short Cuts - Introduction by Todd Cirillo | 7 |
| Perfume & Cigarettes | 9 |
| Why I Meet You at Midnight | 10 |
| Bird's Got My Dream | 12 |
| Catching Lighting | 13 |
| Shooting Stars in the Dark | 14 |
| "My bed's too small for just one us" | 16 |
| Dear Stranger... | 17 |
| Broken Compass | 18 |
| Innocence In A Sense | 20 |
| Fuck Stars | 22 |
| Muse Killer | 23 |
| One Night Stand | 26 |
| My Own Way Home | 27 |
| The Wrong End of Daybreak | 30 |
| Jitter Bed Bugs | 31 |
| The Glass is Always Half Full . . . | 32 |
| My Kind | 33 |
| Maybe Next Time | 34 |
| Wish You Were Here | 35 |
| This One's Just Right | 36 |
| Open 24/7 | 38 |
| Phantom Love | 40 |
| Closing Time | 41 |
| Apple Pie & Cyanide | 42 |
| Stones on My Grave | 44 |
| A Lover's War | 46 |

## No Short Cuts

I am on a porch way up north, a bucket of iced beer next to me, shooting stars above, and crickets accompanying Sam Cooke, singing, "That's where it's at, pretty baby." In my hand is *Perfume & Cigarettes*, and the poet, Madeline Levy, is on my mind. I find myself smiling wickedly to the night and I'm not sure if it's because of the poems in this collection, the beer, or the poet herself—perhaps it's a perfect combination of all three.

This collection is for daytime kissers, "dress code deviants", and late night firearm enthusiasts. It's for those of us who make our own way, because there is "something more beautiful than street signs" to pay attention to in this world. Madeline's images and phrases are: unique, poetic, inviting, sexy, disturbing, vivid, fucking hilarious, difficult, calm, romantic, longing, loving and real. This collection reads like a heart candle, lit in a dark room laying on the floor in a moment that burns on and on.

As a reader, we are left grateful that Madeline did not keep these poems scattered in notebooks to herself. In these poems we hear the roosters crowing at odd hours, we feel the weight of our own hearts while the street signs flash by and streetlights burst on. Her words and experiences make the poetry world a bit more colorful. She is the real deal, no short cuts, no GPS required. One look at these poems will never be enough. They are our poetic presents under the tree, and we cannot wait to open them…again and again. They are the first time she runs her fingers through your hair, that lipstick kiss left on an empty glass…leaving you feeling used and alone, but pleased and strangely satisfied.

So, go ahead and take the long way home down a wrong way street, as Madeline carves *"I am here"* in your heart. I, for one, will happily give her the knife. It's comforting to know she will always be with me, even when she is not.

—Todd Cirillo, poet, editor
1:37a.m., 8/19/15

## Perfume & Cigarettes

The memory of you lingers.
Absorbed in thin skin,
clinging to strands of hair,
like the perfume and cigarettes
I smell in dance clubs
when groups of giggling girls,
in flashy, barely covering clothing,
flip their pretty ponytails
as they walk by.
But when it's drenched
in my own party dress,
tangled in my unbrushed hair
in the sober sunlight,
the smell,
ain't so sweet.

## Why I Meet You at Midnight

I'm not afraid of broken promises,
car windows,
or jaws.

I'm not scared
of all night arguments,
blow out fights,
restraining orders
that always end in promises
made to break.

I don't look over at you,
hoping you'll never rip my heart in two.
I don't pray you won't leave it black and blue.

I see that fury-filled couple in the late night streets,
spitting insults on cracked pavement,
both claiming the other is too drunk.
Her, cursing his flirty eye,
him, blaming it on her sky-high heels,
saying they would both be happier
if she was more...
comfortable.

They don't scare me.
Or make me wish I never become them.

Because nothing's worse
than an empty date,
not even a bad one.
Even listening to a heart broken
and a heartbreaker
sharing stories of their exes

would be better
than hearing the tapping of fake text messages,
pregnant awkward moments,
way past their due date,
as two wordless warriors
surrender to the silence,
waving their hand for the check before dessert
like white flags—
accepting their defeat.

It's why I meet you at midnight,
after my third drink
to join you for the fourth.

Not caring what you say
as long as you're saying it.

I pray we never fall silent
under dim mood lighting,
over salmon and salad,
and an adult glass of wine.

So meet me at midnight

in the back of the bar,
with a bottle of bourbon.

And kiss me
in the morning,

on my way
out the door.

## Bird's Got My Dream

The morning after
the night I got a parrot
I found out
that I talk in my sleep.

He said your name
over and over,
as I sipped
my tea.

## Catching Lighting

In every relationship
there's a lightning bug
flying in a jar

and there's a hand
closing the lid.

## Shooting Stars in the Dark

Yesterday's whirlwind
of flashing beauty
left me breathless.
Lights and music pumping
from the street's stage.
Flowing dresses dancing,
as we watched atop a barstool,
resting for a moment
among the chaos.

The sea of dresses danced
like the flowing body of water
we watched pour
out of Mississippi's mouth,
like my tongue
poured into yours,
the day you put your hands down my pants
and we sat in the sunshine
drinking beer
and burning.

Tonight we can sit on the dock
of your living room couch.
Watch the blood flow
through each other's veins.

We'll match our heartbeats
to the tapping
of your upstairs neighbor's
high-heeled shoes.

When my eyelids fall heavy,
giving in to closing time—
you can walk me home,
up the mountainside of your bed,
where we will lay on our backs
and watch stars shoot
inside our eyelids.

With every goodnight kiss
I will wish
for one more.

## "My bed's too small for just one us"

*- a text message received*

Even now,
as I'm biking away
with hygiene, laundry and logic pointing me
to the direction of my home,
your words
pull me back
to yours.

## Dear Stranger...

I saw you writing one afternoon.

Hunchbacked and hurried—
hungry to spill your guts
onto the tiny pages
that didn't seem to hold
your weight.

I wanted to say something—
anything.
Instead,
I sat there
in silence
and just watched you
fill each unlistening page—
imagining every word
dropping off
like cigarettes
in the
       w
           i
              n
                  d.

## Broken Compass

I'm sorry I kept telling you
how to love me.
You were doing just fine.

We always had chemistry.
We were an ionic bond
that forms
by the attraction
of oppositely charged atoms.

You never asked for my history,
but I told you anyway.
All the nitty gritty—
the victories and defeats,
every inch of land
I discovered
and each small step
I walked
over every man
who tried to claim me.

My fight for independence
and my slide
into The Great Depression.

When you
put up your flag,
and etched "I am here"
into my heart
you didn't need a map.
You knew the route,
but I couldn't stop
giving you directions.

I didn't realize then
that you were always there
and I was the one
who was lost
all along.

I know you didn't need me
to show you
how to love.

But you know what they say,
those who can't *do*—
**teach.**

## Innocence In A Sense

We are not those back alley kissers,
waving around passion
like a five-dollar tip
for an unfazed bartender.

We're not those wide-mouthed,
wild tongue warriors that we pass
with a hint of envy,
as you fumble nervously for my hand
for the first time that evening,
and ask where I'd like to go.

We glare while they revert into adolescence,
hungrily grasping any bit of flesh they can.
We smell their wanting.
You say I look pretty.

We are
those daytime
sidewalk kissers
that families pass when the sun's shining,
after I read a poem I wrote just for you,
and you grab me gently
like I'm as delicate as a promise.

And you smile,
and say my name,
and kiss my lips.
And we revert to adolescence,
not because of the hormones,
but because of the innocence.

Yeah, that's us,
the daytime pinky-linking pair,
with your left hand in my back pocket,
and my red lipstick
staining your right cheek,

as innocent as a goodnight kiss.

## Fuck Stars

when we kissed

I saw

guns

shooting.

## Muse Killer

I'm leaving you.

Before you—
my empty nights
filled my pages
with solemn stories,
with one night stands
followed by
walk-of-shame poems.
Heartbreak harmonies,
whiskey stained,
cigarette burnt
real life inspired
perfumed pieces
that could only be achieved
in non voluntary solitude.
Liberating isolation.

And then there was you.

With kind eyes,
and stability.
Crushing
nothing but the spider in my shower.

So I have to leave you.

If Emily Dickinson got hitched
she wouldn't have written shit.
Nothing's cool about moonlight walks
when you're walking them
with someone else
side by side
in comfortable silence.

No one wants to read
about happy normalcy.

Love is a buzz kill.

Who wants to write
about a perfect date?
No one wants to get drunk
and go dancing
with the girl
who won't stop
talking about her boyfriend
and smiling.

As a friend once said,
"Romance is so nauseating
when it's happening
to someone else."

So I'll trade
telling you my dreams
in the morning
for nightmares
all night long.

Because heartbreak is a killer muse,

and you

are a muse killer.

Because when I look into your eyes
and I think a beautiful thought,
it never hits a page.
It just falls out of my mouth
onto yours,

whispers in your ear,
sinks into your skin
and perishes
before reaching
the pillowcase.

Only the lonely write.
If someone was there to listen—
no one would need
to write
it down.

## One Night Stand

It was a hit and run.
You didn't even leave a note.
And I sure as hell
don't have the type of insurance,
to cover
all the damages.

## My Own Way Home


People tell me I always get lost
like it's a defect,
like it's a problem I should fix.

But what if it's because I'm too busy
looking at something more beautiful
than street signs,
more important
than numbers on houses.

I get lost
watching dancing tree shadows
sway on the pavement
with each breath of air.

I spend more time memorizing
the coarse face of my neighbor,
the curve on the side of his eyes when he smiles,
the tattered cut on his brow—
than remembering
the turns I need to take.

I know I'm going in the right direction
when I see that shabby house
with the bright red door
that shines with grace,
or smell cherry cigars
that burn in the hands
of poker-playing men
who blow smoke rings
across the street.

What if we all felt like tourists
in our own city?

What if we all peeked into souvenir shops,
impulsively scanning corny shot glasses?
Or still waited in long sweaty lines
because whatever's at the end of it
must be worth it, right?

I take bike tours that pass by my house
just to see it from another angle.
I still send postcards,
with trumpets and landmarks,
that say *wish you were here*
instead of homesick letters.

So what
if I ask
for the 20th time
where Burgundy street is?

No matter how many people I love
live there.
No matter how many times I ride my bike
down that street,
I never know the way by heart.

But I always recognize my favorite porch on the way.
The one with the rusty bench that whistles when it swings,
and the old lady that rocks
sipping sweet tea,
who calls me sweetie,
because she doesn't know my name.

And I always remember to wave and say *hey*,
to every messy-haired kid
playing ball in their driveway.

I may still look at my license
every time someone asks where I live.
I never remember the zip code.
But I know it smells like orange in the morning
and glows with street lights in the evening.

I never know the short cuts.
Maybe I secretly like the long way.

Maybe I like riding down the wrong street.
Maybe I think it's better
to feel unfamiliar,
to get off track.
To feel like it's all new
in a city that would feel so old
if I knew it like the back of my hand.

No one ever looked at the back of their hand
and thought,
"wow, that's cool."

Next time I say
I know something
by heart—
you better believe
I don't mean
like the back of my hand.

So I'll stay lost.
Keep your GPS signals.
And I'll take that extra 20 minutes
discovering my way home again.

## The Wrong End of Daybreak

There's a rooster down the street,
always crowing at sunset.
I know how it feels—
all mixed up.

## Jitter Bed Bugs

Drinking coffee at 12 am

like we used to,
out of cracked coffee cups,
even on Monday nights.

Shaking, holding hands,
holding smoking
menthol cigarettes
out of cracked windows
way past the filter.
Trainspotting playing
on repeat with the sound cranked up
so loud,
we could barely hear
our racing thoughts.

Drinking coffee at 12 am.
It just ain't as fun
jittering in bed

all alone.

## The Glass is Always Half Full When it's Not Around

As I drove through the interstates,
I fell in love with you.

Your annoying habits
became endearing.
I started to admire the way
you yelled in public,
your awful taste in music,
how you'd press the snooze button
ten times
each morning
on the loudest alarm clock
ever.
Started to miss
closing the toothpaste cap
every morning.

I had to cross
the Mason-Dixon Line
to realize
how beautiful you are

when I'm leaving.

## My Kind

Forget the pretty birds,
I go for the film-coated city
daytime bats, the radical-winged rats.
Not the chicks pecking
on the rationed bread crumb.
Or the ones gliding into
pastel colored
crystal-cup cafes
boldly,
and the dumpsters
in the back
shamelessly.
You don't find my kind printed on postcards—
basking in palm trees.
They'll be dodging a taxi
on Fifth Ave.
Fighting their own
for trash-filled
tuna fish.
Sleeping next to
Parisian bums
under flickering florescent streetlights.
Flattened under unforgiving tires.

Yeah, that's my kind.
The not-too-proud-to beg.
The never-too-dark-to-fly.
The dress code deviants.
Uninvited guests.
Those are the ones for me.
The ones with rain absorbed
in their black feathers,
and what looks like a wicked smile
spread across
their dirty beaks.

## Maybe Next Time

As "I Would do Anything for Love"
by Meatloaf
blared through the boombox
in my brain

I wondered
what I could have done
for love.

Wondered if the one thing
he
couldn't do

was let her go.

## Wish You Were Here

Here is where
I wish you were.

But if you were,

it still
wouldn't be
enough.

## This One's Just Right

Lovers are like keys.

So many close to fitting
but only one is
just right.
Each lock,
like Goldi's lock,
she just knew
as soon as the porridge
touched her lips,
and her head hit just the right bed,
Goldi's lock
opened.

I, too,
touched too many
too soft,
too hard,
too cold and
too hot,
in my search
for the perfect fit.

I have a whole chain
filled with keys.
Slightly faulty,
almost-perfect,
half-inserted fits.

I pushed
harder and harder,
convinced it was
the one.

I clogged the latch,
blocking the bolt,
certain
that if I just tried
a little longer,
if I twisted it
just right,
it would unlock.

So many nights
I climbed through my own window,
lost the keys
that didn't work anyway.
I was convinced my lock
was broken.

I didn't realize
it wasn't the lock—
but the keys,

until you let me in.

## Open 24/7

On those cool, foggy nights,
I let the door swing half open,
look down at my cat
who's lookin' right up at me,
wide-eyed
and shaky-tailed.

Outside looks alright—
not the type of cold that'll bite
or the warmth that begs for her footsteps,
just a normal misty evening
full of uncertainty.
So she takes a look,
taps her foot on the cement front step,
turns around and rubs my leg.
I think to myself—
this is what love is,
looking out of a half open door
to a side that don't look half bad,
but turning around,
and choosing
to stay.

I hope you'll always leave
a shimmer of the moonlight
seeping through the cracks
of your iron gate.
I know that I can always
jump over,
even though every time I leave
I skin my bones;
I always come back.

I'll leave two welcome mats—
one pointing to the front door

so you never hesitate
when it's been so long
since you've been around,
that you'll wonder if I've changed
the locks.
And one in reverse
so you know—
the world will welcome you, too,
and you'll know I approve.

I'll leave my door half open,
even on nights
when your head is on my pillow
and I'll be here
hoping
I'm on your favorite side.

## Phantom Love

I miss you in my bed.
The way my fingers reach for the necklace
I lost in that gas station
we stopped at in Michigan
for Red Bull and beef jerky,
reaching for your hand
like I would an amputated limb
I never needed.
I check my phone for your call,
the way I check my empty refrigerator
10 times.
Each time expecting it to be full
of leftover pizza,
unspoiled milk,
or
*I'm sorry,*
*please come back* messages.

Maybe if I stop setting the table for two,
and sleep on what was once your side of the bed,
I will soon
no longer
reach for you in the morning.

## Closing Time

*To all the bands we can't remember, and their songs we'll never forget*

You're just a one hit wonder, baby,
and I was the 15 minutes of fame.

You gave up

because you didn't know
it was your last
shot.

## Apple Pie & Cyanide

I haven't written a decent poem
since you left.
I wanted to make something
beautiful,

but I just kept writing your name.

I once heard that apple seeds have cyanide.
That if you eat enough apple seeds,
the cyanide
will kill you.

It would take 5 milligrams.
Each seed has .6.

The day you left
I baked a pie
out of a hundred apples,
topped it with cyanide seed sprinkles,
washed it down
with a tall glass
of apple core juice.

I waited and waited.

The poison pie
wouldn't drag me
six feet under.

But inside I grew
an apple tree
so big,

it tore through my belly,
branched out in my bedroom,
ripped open the roof,

until all I saw was sky.

At least now
I'll have a shady spot
to sit
and wait
for you to come back.

And if you don't,
at least I made
something beautiful
after all.

## Stones on My Grave

*influenced by Jagger and Richards*

I often think about what they'll say
at my funeral.
In black pressed slacks, modest dresses and shiny shoes,
over microwaved hors d'oeuvres,
between whispered claims that I'm in a "better place."

I imagine what words
they will choose
to describe me.

"She was a strong
coffee drinker"...
"She was a great
tipper"...
"an awful singer"...
"But she sure had enthusiasm!"

I wonder what character defects
someone will spin
into cheeky rhetoric,
convincing the mourning audience that it was endearing
the way I never answered the phone,
how I left the cupboard doors wide open,
forgot birthdays,
and always lost my keys.

I imagine what nostalgia-drenched memory will have its glory
dripping out of an old friend's mouth,
sounding better
than the day it happened,

because stories sound better than memories feel—
most of the time.

I wonder what old lovers will wait in line
to see my face for the last time.
Which ones will cry,
or silently confess
that they loved me the best.
Which ones will curse me
for giving up,
or leaving,
or never coming back.

But what I really wonder,
is who will bring me dead flowers,
and won't forget
to put roses
on my grave.

## A Lover's War

Before leaving,
I put a letter
in your memory-shaped mailbox,
and kept the edges sharp
so you can open it
when I'm gone.
It will leave a paper-sized cut
in the back of your heart,
a vacant space,
filled with a ghost of pain—
a tiny reminder
that our love
is still bleeding,
that the battle scars
are just healing,
that no war
is more dangerous
than a lover's war.

**Madeline Levy** is a Jersey belle just trying to make it in the Big Easy. She's been referred to as a mix between a "manic, pixie dream girl" and a "happy, harpy nap lady." She can be found reading her poetry in front of half-lit New Orleans folks, in the back of dimly-lit barrooms where jukeboxes play loud enough to make a soundtrack for her set.

*Perfume & Cigarettes* is her first collection of poetry.

## Thanks to:

To Six Ft. Swells crew Julie and Matt for the praise and criticism, countless back and forth emails, and patience that I needed so. Your vigorous honesty, irrefutable talent, and bold nature has inspired, and made this book possible.

Special thanks to Todd for the push I needed, that at times felt like a shove. Thanks for putting up with my crazy, and showing me yours. For the aggressive faith and inspiration that without, these poems would have never left my laptop.

Allie, Carlee and Sihem, for being my best friends, miles and months away from each other.

Ben, for inspiring and influencing me in ways you may not know. I'd probably suck without you, and have really bad taste in music.

Jesse, for always doing what you want, usually knowing what that is, following pipe dreams, and never getting a real job, "Why would anyone want a job? Life's too short to have a job." —Ghost Mice

And my parents… of course.
My mom. For literally everything. And for showing me to appreciate beauty.

My Paw, for the strange humor you've unleashed into the world, and instilled in your children.

www.ingramcontent.com/pod-product-compliance
Lightning Source LLC
Chambersburg PA
CBHW071801040426
42446CB00012B/2657